Are Aliens Real?

BY PATRICK PERISH

amicus
high interest

Amicus High Interest is published by Amicus
P.O. Box 1329, Mankato, MN 56002
www.amicuspublishing.us

Library of Congress Cataloging-in-Publication Data
Perish, Patrick.
 Are aliens real? / Patrick Perish.
   p. cm. — (Unexplained, what's the evidence?)
 Audience: K to grade 3
  Includes index.
Summary: "Presents famous alien stories and briefly examines the
claims, ultimately stating there is no hard proof of aliens"—Provided by
publisher.
 ISBN 978-1-60753-383-2 (library binding) —
ISBN 978-1-60753-431-0 (ebook)
1. Extraterrestrial beings—Juvenile literature. 2. Quacks and
quackery—Juvenile literature. I. Title.
 QB54.P45 2014
 001.942—dc23
                    2012036391

Editor: Rebecca Glaser
Designer: Kathleen Petelinsek

Photo Credits: Alamy/Friedrich Saurer, 9; Alamy/Jon Arnold Images
Ltd, 12-13; Alamy/M L Pearson, 18; Alamy/Mary Evans Picture
Library, 17; Corbis/AP Photo/Ben Margot, 26; Corbis/Bettmann,
14, 22; Corbis/Imaginechina, 6-7; Corbis/Robin Loznak, 25;
NASA, 5; NASA/JPL/Caltech, 29; Shutterstock/Chris Harvey, cover;
Shutterstock/photobank.kiev.ua, 21; Shutterstock/Tero Hakala, 10

Printed in the United States at Corporate Graphics in
North Mankato, Minnesota.
4/2014/1221
10 9 8 7 6 5

Table of Contents

What are Aliens?

Look at the night sky. There are more stars than grains of sand on all the world's beaches. Planets **orbit** many of those stars. Could aliens live out there? Aliens are creatures from other planets.

Could aliens live far away in outer space?

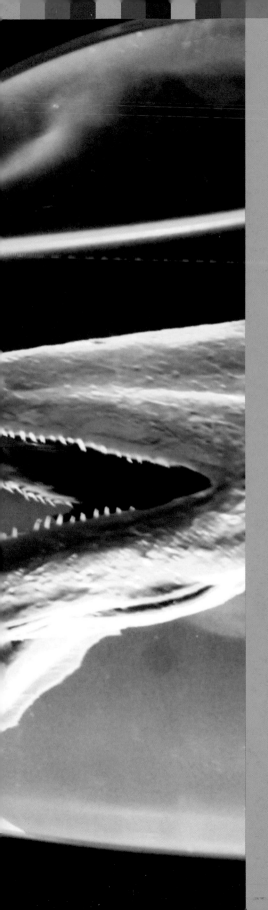

There is no hard proof of aliens. But there are strange stories! Many people say they've met aliens. Some are friendly. Other stories tell about aliens that capture people. Many alien stories are made up. Others can't be explained.

Could aliens look like sea creatures? Maybe!

Aliens don't all look the same. Some are strange! **Grays** are the most common. They have big heads and huge eyes. Their skin is smooth and gray. Nordic aliens look like humans. They are tall. They have blond hair and blue eyes. They are friendly. Some aliens look like giant bugs or lizards.

Many reports of aliens tell about "grays." But there is no proof that they are real.

9

Humans built the large statues on Easter Island, not aliens.

First Reports

Could aliens have visited Earth long ago? Some people think so. Aliens might have built ancient places like the pyramids. The rocks for Stonehenge came from far away. The Easter Island statues weigh over 80 tons (73 metric tons). All these were built before cranes or trucks. But scientists have proved humans built them! Wow!

The Dogon tribe lives in Africa. The Dogon know all about the faraway star Sirius B. You need a **telescope** to see it from Earth. But the Dogon don't have telescopes! How did they learn about that star? Their legends say fish-like aliens came. The aliens taught their ancestors about space.

The Dogon are known for their masks.

Betty and Barney Hill wrote a book about how they were kidnapped by aliens.

 **Q** How does a **trance** help?

Alien Stories

It was 1961. Betty and Barney Hill were driving home. They saw a weird light in the night sky. They stopped. Barney saw a spaceship. Suddenly, they were miles down the road. But the Hills didn't remember what happened. Later, a doctor put them into a trance. They remembered being captured by aliens!

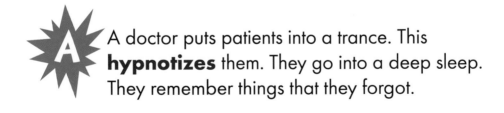

A doctor puts patients into a trance. This **hypnotizes** them. They go into a deep sleep. They remember things that they forgot.

George Adamski had a message. Aliens were real. He had met one. In the 1950s, many people said they met aliens. They were called **contactees**. They thought the aliens chose them. The aliens took them on trips. They went to Mars, Venus, and the Moon. Later, scientists proved this could not happen.

Why might contactees make up stories about aliens?

Adamski is next to a painting of a space pilot. He said they met in 1952.

 One reason is to feel important. Aliens are big news. Another reason is to make money. Alien stories often get made into books or movies.

Newspapers reported the Roswell crash. But a general said it was just a weather balloon.

The most famous alien story took place at Roswell, New Mexico. In 1947, a rancher found a strange crash site. The Air Force sent a team to see what crashed. They took all the pieces to study. They said a weather balloon had crashed. But later, **witnesses** said they saw aliens at the crash site. No one knows for sure what crashed at Roswell.

In 1975, loggers in Arizona met aliens. Travis Walton and his crew were going home. They saw strange lights. Travis went close. Buzz! A beam of light hit him. It knocked him back several feet! His scared crew drove off. Travis disappeared. He returned five days later. He said he was taken onto a spaceship. He saw aliens. Later they let him go.

Did an alien spaceship like this one really capture Travis Walton? Only he knows for sure.

Exposing the Fakes

Many alien stories turn out to be false. Some are fakes. Others were never meant to be real. In 1938, Orson Welles put on a radio play. It was about an alien landing. The show was told like a news report. Some people tuned in late. They thought aliens really landed in America! They panicked.

Orson Welles practices his fiction radio play, "The War of the Worlds." Some people thought it was real.

In 1995, Ray Santilli found an old video. It was from the Roswell crash. The video showed doctors looking at a dead body. It was an alien! Some people said it was proof. The government was hiding facts! But in 2006, Santilli said the video was fake. He said it was based on a real video. But the real tape had fallen apart.

 How was the fake alien body made?

This movie prop is from a TV movie about the Roswell crash.

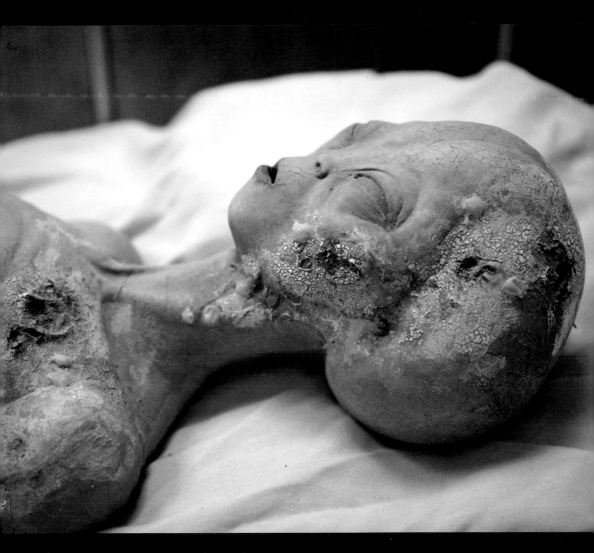

 Santilli and his friends used art supplies to make a body. They filled it with chicken and sheep parts from a butcher.

SETI has huge telescopes
in California that scan for
signs of alien life.

 **Q** Who looks for aliens?

What's the Evidence?

The universe is big. Many scientists believe there are other planets like Earth. Some are older than ours. They could be home to alien life. But the only proof for aliens comes from stories. Alien witnesses think they are telling the truth. But without hard proof, no one knows for sure.

 The SETI Institute looks for aliens. Their name stands for the Search for Extraterrestrial Intelligence. They listen for radio signals from aliens.

In August 2012, scientists put a rover on Mars. They want to see if Mars once had life. The rover moves slowly. It tests the air and soil. It takes pictures. Maybe it will find proof. Maybe it won't. There is no hard proof for aliens yet. But there are many strange stories. What do you think?

 How many planets like Earth are there?

**This rover is looking
for signs of life on Mars.**

 One professor estimates that 100 million
planets in our **galaxy** could have life!

Glossary

contactee A person who claims to have been visited by aliens.

galaxy A very large group of stars and planets.

Gray The most common type of reported alien, with gray skin and a large head.

hypnotize To put someone into a deep sleep where they don't know what's happening around them.

orbit To travel around a planet or star in a circular or oval-shaped path.

telescope A tool for looking at things in outer space.

trance A deep sleep that can help people remember things they have forgotten.

witness A person who has seen an event take place.

Read More

Bolstrood, Gomer. *The Alien Hunter's Guide*. Monster Tracker. Mankato, Minn.: Sea-to-Sea Publications, 2012.

Erickson, Justin. *Alien Abductions.* The Unexplained. Minneapolis: Bellwether Media, 2011.

Halls, Kelly Milner. *Alien Investigation, Searching for the Truth about UFOs and Aliens*. Minneapolis: Millbrook Press, 2012.

Websites

The Official Travis Walton Website
http://www.travis-walton.com/

SETI Institute
http://www.seti.org/

UFO Casebook
http://www.ufocasebook.com/

UFO Evidence: Selected Cases
http://www.ufoevidence.org/cases/ufocaseshome.asp

Index

About the Author

Patrick Perish spent many childhood nights under the covers with a flashlight and good book. In particular, aliens, ghosts, and other unexplained mysteries have always kept him up until the wee hours of the night. He lives in Minneapolis, MN where he writes and edits children's books.